Raúl Norambuena Naguil

Draft of a new Political Constitution of the Republic of Chile

AF209886

Raúl Norambuena Naguil

Draft of a new Political Constitution of the Republic of Chile

A vision of the future for 21st century Chile

ScienciaScripts

Imprint
Any brand names and product names mentioned in this book are subject to trademark, brand or patent protection and are trademarks or registered trademarks of their respective holders. The use of brand names, product names, common names, trade names, product descriptions etc. even without a particular marking in this work is in no way to be construed to mean that such names may be regarded as unrestricted in respect of trademark and brand protection legislation and could thus be used by anyone.

Cover image: www.ingimage.com

This book is a translation from the original published under ISBN 978-620-3-03398-4.

Publisher:
Sciencia Scripts
is a trademark of
Dodo Books Indian Ocean Ltd. and OmniScriptum S.R.L publishing group

120 High Road, East Finchley, London, N2 9ED, United Kingdom
Str. Armeneasca 28/1, office 1, Chisinau MD-2012, Republic of Moldova, Europe
Managing Directors: Ieva Konstantinova, Victoria Ursu
info@omniscriptum.com

Printed at: see last page
ISBN: 978-620-3-39355-2

Copyright © Raúl Norambuena Naguil
Copyright © 2021 Dodo Books Indian Ocean Ltd. and OmniScriptum S.R.L publishing group

Acknowledgements

I would like to give special recognition and thanks to the following people, especially for having contributed to my gaining more knowledge or for having supported me and thus making this ambitious project to improve the lives of all people in this country possible:

Pedro Hernán Larrère Castro, notary;

Hernán Beltrán Silva, director S.K.I.F.;

Raúl Norambuena Vidal, chartered

accountant; Ricardo Andrés Loyola,

lawyer;

Manabu Murakami, political

scientist; Hirokazu Kanazawa, *soke*;

Nobuaki Kanazawa, *kancho*;

Antonio Morales Manzo, lawyer;

Jorge Sandrock Carrasco, lawyer;

Felipe Harrison Eyquem, lawyer;

Nicole Darat Guerra, philosopher;

Paulina Puentes Jorge, actress and speech

therapist; Eduardo Court Murasso, lawyer;

Juan Pablo Cox Leixelard, lawyer;

Felipe de la Fuente Hulaud, lawyer;

Sebastián Figueroa Rubio, lawyer;

Sophía Romero Rodríguez, lawyer;

Patricia Lorca Riofrio, lawyer;

Carolina Salinas García, lawyer;

Felipe Sepúlveda González,

professor;

Chile, its constitutions and a new vision of the future.

Chile's constitutional history is interesting to analyse, as it runs along a path that is at times broken and at other times more even, making it look like a kind of stream in the middle of a rugged and enormous geography with great reliefs and valleys. Since the early days of our country's organisation, it has wanted to have a Fundamental Charter to mark the destiny of a nation in constant change and in need of a legal pillar to support it.

Initially, the idea was to safeguard the interests of King Ferdinand VII, who had been disgraced by the French invasion, a paradigm that soon gave way to faint sparks of libertarian revolution interrupted by the advance of the royalist restorationist forces that imposed the monarchical order once again. However, after the emancipation struggles, the Supreme Director, Don Bernardo O'Higgins felt it was necessary to provide the country with a Magna Carta that would mark a break with the old institutionality, breaking the subject-king relationship and moving on to that of State-citizen, with equal conditions and strengthening the channels, which by then, democracy knew.

The first two, those of 1818 and 1822, were drafted under the leadership of Supreme Director O'Higgins, who appointed people to help him draft these legal bodies, which were short-lived. They were followed by that of 1823, the work of Juan Egaña, who worked together with a Constituent Congress which was the body responsible for carrying forward the drafting of a new constitution for Chile, but which in the end left everything in the hands of such an illustrious character, although his work did not have the stability that was expected, since the attempts of José Miguel Infante to establish a federal state in Chile in 1826, undermined the normative capacity of the 1823 charter. In my personal opinion, perhaps the best option for this Republic could have been federal laws, but the country at that time was not ready to join such a complex system as the federal one, which today, in the 21st century, seems to be the most viable alternative.

After this Constitution of 1823 and the federal laws, which were never an organised body, came the Constitution of 1828, also created from a Constituent Congress whose goal was to create a "popular representative republican" constitution, which was finally written by the fine pen of a man of literature from Cadiz, Don José Joaquín de Mora y Sánchez, famous author, among other works, of the "Meditaciones Poéticas" which contained twelve original poems inspired by the engravings made by William Blake for Robert Blair's poem: "The Grave", published in London in 1826.

Despite such an important and illustrious pen, the Constitution of 1828 was not able to withstand the political ups and downs and the struggle between the liberal and conservative sides, falling after the battle of Lircay, which gave rise to the oldest constitution the country ever had, that of 1833, which was inspired by the philosophy of the minister Portales and drafted by the liberal Manuel José Gandarillas and the conservative Mariano Egaña. This constitution was the one that most strongly resisted the political, economic and military onslaughts in which our country was confronted, and which did not escape the turbulence in which the other American countries were involved. In short, it was able to face the assassination of a Minister of State, the Celopathic wars against the Peruvian-Bolivian Confederation, the Chilean invasion of Bolivia that triggered the Saltpetre War, the Revolutions of 1855, 1859 and the cruel one of 1891, Spain's attack on its former American dominions, the Catholic Church's internal struggle against the State and a de facto pseudo-parliamentary regime installed at the end of the 19th century.

It is this last milestone, the de facto pseudo-parliamentary regime that broke the constitution in 1925, which after a series of pressures that even drove Arturo Alessandri from the presidency, was changed by the charter of the same year, which was prepared by an assembly of representatives of all the political parties (from conservatives to communists), social organisations and the army; it was then submitted to a plebiscite to come into force on 18 September 1925.

However, despite the cohesion of so many heterogeneous thoughts, this new constitution was not able to face the onslaught of a world very different from the one that gave it life. The installation of the Cold War in the world caused the constitution to collapse in a Chile intervened by North American interests that would not allow President Salvador Allende to govern and provoked the 1973 coup d'état. This marked the end of the 1925 Charter, which had already seen part of its end with a draft constitution of the People's Government, which laid the fundamental pillars on which the road to socialism in Chile would be built, a project which, as we know, never saw the light of day.

After the 1973 coup d'état, the idea of drafting a Fundamental Charter began to take shape.

4

that stamped the seal of a "never again" for a left-wing government, proposing the free market and opening the country to the cruelest and bloodiest capitalism. Thus the 1980 Constitution was born, on the basis of a commission formed for the purpose and guided by the intellects of Don Enrique Ortúzar, Jaime Guzmán, Enrique Evans de la Cuadra, Alejandro Silva Bascuñán, Sergio Diez Urzúa, among others.

The 1980 constitution governed under a transitory form until 1989, then it began to govern fully until the year 2019, when a social revolt managed to position a process of "revolution" in Chile, which remains to this day. One of the major milestones of this revolution was to impose the idea of a referendum to decide how to change the constitution, which resulted in the formation of a Constituent Commission, made up of democratically elected citizens, which will draft the final text to be submitted for popular approval.

This is, roughly speaking, part of the constitutional history of this country and, as will be seen, behind a body of constitutional law there is always a person, an ideologist who gives life to that law. Well, what we have today in the 21st century is a draft Magna Carta by someone who could be Egaña, Infante, Gandarillas or any other name of the most respectable 19th century jurist to whom we owe the organisation of a country in the midst of the process of republican freedom.

Regardless of the ideological stance with which the constitution proposed by the author can be analysed, it is a contribution of enormous value, not only for the academic world, but also for the country in general, since it demonstrates the thinking of the young generations who have wanted to change this country and who have designed in their still dreamy minds what the country they will bequeath to the future will be like.

A State needs to have a normative structure and what better if this structure carries the inspiration of the future inhabitants of the country, who in this case of our author, is a young promise of legal thought who, from the far south, illuminates with his dream of a better world, blessed youthful hope, the steps that this nation must take to organise itself in order to promote the common good.

From a brief analysis of its articles, the proposal appears to be novel and up-to-date in terms of concepts, although it maintains the unitary state structure and does not make the powerful leap to federalism, it reflects the change from the paradigm of the absent state to a more powerful and close to the citizenship forgotten since the 70s of the 20th century. The novel enumeration of fundamental rights brings Chile up to date with the defence, less and less present, of the prerogatives of each and every one of us free citizens of the country, in short, an interesting text that deserves to be inscribed in the constitutional history that is being written down today, this new constitutional essay.

Ricardo Andrés Loyola
Professor of History of Law
Adolfo Ibáñez University
Chile

Preamble

The present draft of the Political Constitution of the Republic is a representation of the need of the State of Chile to legitimise democracy materially, achieving the great step from a neo-liberal Constitution made during a military dictatorship towards a Democratic Constitution that guarantees the rights that the people should always possess to be exercised freely.

The Constitutions of various states around the world, such as Germany, Spain, Bolivia, Japan, Portugal, Russia, among others, have been used as references, as well as international treaties on human rights, assemblies held in conjunction with citizens and the doctrine of various authors. This Constitution prescribes the highest international human rights standards and is the work of a social Constitution.

Today, democracy can leave aside the distrustful, dissatisfied and exhausted step to start its firm, vigilant, satisfied, happy, fighting and enthusiastic step, because it is not just a vague idea, we can by no means look at it from a distance, we must never believe that it is just a project; because with a little will we can achieve changes, with hope in the future we will allow ourselves to create it and together working to improve we will reach every goal set: this is the Political Constitution of the New Republic.

In the following, I will briefly outline the new issues raised by my draft Constitution, some of the differences with the current one, and other concise explanations.

The first notable difference with respect to the current Constitution is in one aspect of form. Unlike the current Constitution, which begins with a chapter entitled: "Bases of Institutionality", the Constitution I propose begins immediately with the chapter: "Fundamental Rights and Guarantees", which are basically those known as "human rights".

Article 2 guarantees the right to life, just as it does today, but adds

It also guarantees a "life with dignity" and removes the death penalty from our legal system. Furthermore, it allows euthanasia and abortion to be established by law only, while respecting human dignity at all times. In this way, euthanasia and abortion cannot be legislated as a criminal sanction or as a reproach to an individual or a sector of society, as well as not proceeding in the case of arbitrary discrimination.

Article 3 guarantees physical integrity and prohibits torture and all types of unlawful coercion, in addition to clearly prescribing respect for international treaties signed by Chile and the law.

Article 4 guarantees the right to psychological integrity. Something new is given in the fact that: "The State shall endeavour to provide the means for the good mental health of its inhabitants" and that: "The State recognises the right of everyone to the enjoyment of the highest attainable standard of mental health", issues that are not currently established.

Article 5 guarantees the right to be forgotten. Although up to now case law has been enshrining it, deriving from the right to honour, to psychological integrity and the right to ownership of one's image, also a matter of doctrine and case law, also established in comparative law, this is a new right prescribed from now on and forever in our constitutional order.

Article 6 guarantees equality before the law, which already exists, but with the substantial modification that the state shall promote the elimination of the existing disadvantages between men and women. At present, both are simply recognised as equal before the law, but now, in addition to enshrining this, what is actually happening and what needs to be eliminated is also being considered. In this way, we will move towards a society with effective equality between men and women with equal pay for equal work.

equal opportunities to access jobs under the same conditions and without discrimination, among other situations.

Article 7 enshrines equality before the law and the prohibition of arbitrary discrimination. A novel point is to state that: "persons belonging to ethnic, religious or linguistic minorities shall not be denied the right, in community with the other members of their group, to enjoy their own cultural life, to profess and practise their own religion and to use their own language". In this way, the cultural expression of the minorities existing in our country is guaranteed, among other issues, which are also constitutionally guaranteed.

Article 9 enshrines numerous guarantees for defendants. Furthermore, it establishes the right of all persons to a free lawyer, provided that they cannot afford one, not only for criminal defendants, but also in any other area of law, and not only to represent them in court, since this right will also exist to provide advice. Penalties for minors will at all times take into consideration their social reintegration. In addition, greater guarantees are given to persons unjustly convicted so that they can obtain compensation from the State for all damages, whether for the time they were unable to work, the things they lost or the psychological suffering they suffered, among others.

Article 10 enshrines the state's obligation to facilitate the social reintegration of persons who have been convicted, thus contributing to the reduction of crime and the formation of people who are more committed to society.

Article 11 enshrines the right to freedom of movement and the possible restrictions that may be placed by law on this right, only for particularly serious and justified reasons such as imprisonment for a crime or for particularly serious disasters.

Article 12 guarantees the right to migrate. In addition, various measures are enshrined to ensure equal treatment between foreigners and Chileans in relation to education, profession, housing, access to self-managed enterprises and access to life.

and their participation in it. In addition, they shall be protected against exploitation in the field of culture.

The EU should also ensure that we will never again see foreigners renting in conditions that violate human dignity in our country.

Article 13 enshrines the right of assembly and expands the examples of places of public use in order to put an end to doctrinal discussions as to whether they are places of public use or national property for public use, accepting the former doctrine. Furthermore, in relation to the international treaties in force signed by Chile, it is enshrined that only by virtue of a law can this right be limited for the justified reasons stated.

Article 15 enshrines the right to health. The right to medical treatment, which is protected, is new in this Constitution. Furthermore, health in public institutions shall be free of charge in all its forms, health being a human right and not a business. The right to sport is also guaranteed, knowing that it is of utmost importance for physical and mental health.

Article 16 guarantees the right to a pollution-free environment and the obligation to maintain the good state of nature, as well as to ensure the correct use of natural resources, thus prohibiting the depredation of resources. The State shall ensure that this right is not affected: "The law may establish specific restrictions to constitutional rights in order to protect the environment."

Article 17, in addition to the right to honour and privacy of the individual and those close to them, explicitly enshrines the right to one's own image, as well as allowing the use of information technology to be restricted in order to protect the honour and privacy of individuals.

Article 18 enshrines the right to the inviolability of the home and all forms of private communication and also establishes a new right for our legal system: the right to decent and adequate housing of adequate size. Thus, everyone shall have the right to housing that respects the dignity of his or her

being human, which contributes to better mental health and tends to happiness.

of citizens.

Article 19 enshrines religious freedom. Furthermore: "No religious organisation shall receive privileges from the State, nor shall it exercise political authority. No one shall be obliged to take part in religious acts, celebrations, rites or practices of any kind. The State and its agencies shall refrain from intervening in religious education and any other activity of this nature, being a secular State". Being a secular state, the state must withdraw from religious activities, as the separation of church and state must be a reality in the 21st century.

Article 20 enshrines the right to freedom of opinion or freedom of expression and information. Furthermore, "propaganda or agitation inciting social, racial, national or conscientious hatred or hostility shall not be permitted. Propaganda for social, racial, national, religious or linguistic supremacy is prohibited". In a democracy, speech that seeks to end democracy or the rights of others should not be tolerated, and freedom of expression does not mean tolerating speech that does not exist.

Article 22 enshrines the right to education and the constitutionally protected rights of children. It also requires the state to ensure that persons who have not completed basic education are able to obtain fundamental education.

Article 23 enshrines the right to freedom of education in all its forms, including *homeschooling, with the* only limitations being "public order, national security and respect for fundamental rights" and legal regulations.

Article 24, in addition to enshrining the right to free choice of work, establishes the free choice of profession and stresses that all persons must be remunerated without discrimination, which means that, among other examples, a man and a woman may not be paid differently for the same work and experience. The right to rest and leisure is also enshrined. In addition, those who are unable to work are to be protected.

with state support for their livelihoods and the interesting thing about this is that not only those who have

The bill also provides for those who are unable to work due to their financial situation to be entitled to it. It is also proposed that those over 18 years of age who are not studying and are working will be obliged to care for their disabled parents, with exceptions being made on "justified grounds" through a court judgement. These reasons could be, for example, that their parents mistreated them, abandoned them or never took care of them, among others at the discretion of the judge and the law. The right to strike is also enshrined.

Article 25 enshrines the right to organise and that all workers will be able to defend their rights through trade unions. This means that, for example, the law cannot say that there are companies in which trade unions cannot exist because they do not have the minimum number of workers to do so.

Article 26 protects the social and economic rights of Chileans working abroad and policies for their return.

Article 27 enshrines employers' freedom of contract and establishes an exception to this right with the possibility that the law may enshrine it, thus being able to force a person to work when he or she has accepted to do so, through a court sentence. Here we are thinking especially of the criminal sanction of forcing someone to work, in accordance with the social reintegration of the perpetrator of the crime and thus preventing him from committing new crimes.

Article 28 enshrines the right to food, new in our constitutional order and already obligatory for Chile since it signed the international treaties that contain this right. The State will be in charge of providing this right to those who do not have the means to do so for themselves, thus contributing to end hunger in Chile and to enable people to live a more peaceful life for their families, friends, leisure, work, economy and within society in general.

Article 29 enshrines the constitutional right to water, and not only to the granting of water rights, but that everyone has the right to drinking water and that water companies cannot interrupt the service for non-payment if the law says that water must be paid for. This has some consequences: the

The law may establish that it is a free service for everyone or it may establish that it must be paid for; everyone must have access to drinking water, putting an end to thirst in Chile; and companies may not suspend the service, but they may collect the outstanding amount through the corresponding executive or ordinary lawsuit, as established by law.

Article 30 enshrines the right to social security, states that the law may establish compulsory contributions, but also adds that pensioners will have the right of ownership over their contributions, guarantees the economic sufficiency of the elderly and promotes social services that will attend to the problems of health, housing, culture and leisure of pensioners. This establishes the right to economic security for the elderly and brings us one step closer to a fair society for those who have given their lives, thus helping to pay off the debt we owe them as a country.

Article 31 enshrines the right to petition the authority. This may be done individually or collectively by any person, but members of the armed forces may only do so individually, thus preventing pressure being exerted by an institution against any authority or the state itself.

Article 34 enshrines the free economic initiative of any person and establishes that the state may have enterprises with greater facilities than those that currently exist in order to reactivate the economy, provide jobs for people and contribute to the provision of services.

Article 35 enshrines the self-determination of peoples and that the State must protect indigenous peoples, which is a historical debt owed to them.

and a fundamental right that they need to acquire.

Article 36 protects culture, history and archaeology. It also protects those values, including religious values, of existing indigenous peoples such as the Mapuche or extinct ones such as the Inka.

Article 39 enshrines the right to asylum for politically persecuted persons.
In Articles 41 and 42, the actions for protection and amparo are maintained, with the corresponding extensions in protected rights and thus highlighting the greater possibility of protecting the environment.

Article 46 of Chapter II enshrines the right of resistance of all Chileans against those who attempt to eliminate the democratic order of Chile, as long as there are no other remedies before, the right of resistance being a last resort to protect our freedom, democracy and fundamental rights provided for by this new Constitution.

Article 47 enshrines that the state protects not only human life, but also animals.

Article 48 enshrines the scope of international law in our state.

Article 49, while stating that Chile is a unitary state, also recognises that within it there is a plurality of peoples and that the state shall promote local identification and indigenous peoples in their respective geographical areas.

Article 51, regarding political parties, stipulates in the second paragraph that: "parties that by their aims or by the behaviour of their militants or adherents tend to distort or eliminate the fundamental regime of freedom and democracy, or to endanger the existence of the Republic of Chile, are unconstitutional" and the consequence of those who commit these acts is to prevent them for life from holding any elected office, since our State protects democracy, freedom and constitutional rights and whoever contravenes this should not hold power. Furthermore,

This will be decided by the Supreme Court.

Article 53 states that the armed forces have the obligation to: "guarantee the sovereignty and independence of Chile, defend its territorial integrity and constitutional order". They are in charge of protecting us all, protecting their people and never attacking them. In addition, it is enshrined that the Carabineros and PDI will have the obligation to have quality training, constant education and training and a thorough knowledge of the legislation applicable to their competences. As a result of this,

cases in which judges are forced to release defendants because of a mistake in police procedures will be drastically reduced; the police will be in optimal physical condition to enable them to carry out their duties more easily; and every effort will be made to eradicate the abuse of power by the Carabineros or PDI.

When there is a disaster, such as a major earthquake or tsunami, the president may request the assistance of the armed forces for whatever work is necessary. However, on the fifth day the parliament must decide whether or not to keep them in the relief services for a further five days, and this can be repeated. It should be noted that in these cases only the right of assembly can be restricted, which is due to the effort not to hinder reconstruction, debris removal or similar relief work.

There is also the unlikely possibility of civil war. In this case, the president must obtain parliamentary authorisation to decree the deployment of the armed forces for 30 days, which can be increased by a further 15 days at each vote at the end of the period. It should be mentioned that the authorisation can be revoked by either the president or parliament at any time and that the authorisation will be deemed revoked, in any case, once the danger has ended. The purpose of the authorisation by parliament to deploy the armed forces is to prevent, as far as possible, a situation where the people elect a president who, during his term of office, promotes authoritarian or autocratic ideas and can misuse the army against his people. In such a state, "the rights to freedom of movement, assembly, the inviolability of the home and of all forms of private communication and of property if requisitioning is strictly necessary, which will be fairly compensated afterwards".

In the event of external war or defence in the event of enemy attack, the President shall request authorisation from Parliament to deploy the armed forces. When it is not possible to have the authorisation of the Parliament for the justified reasons mentioned in the article and the attack is imminent, the President shall seek the authorisation of the Ministers.

of State, which may authorise it with 2/3 of their votes. All matters concerning war or national defence shall be regulated by a law with a quorum of 4/7.

Article 55 mentions that innovation and technological advances are indispensable for the proper development of our country, and that the countries that invest the most in these areas are the richest in the world, not only in terms of money or the economy. It also establishes that the State must ensure the correct distribution of wealth, but always respecting constitutional guarantees and the law so as not to harm any person or group in the process.

Article 57 of Chapter II eliminates the distinctions between the terms "Chilean" and "citizen" that currently exist, and Article 59 establishes that from the age of 18 the right to vote and to be elected in popular elections may be exercised, without prejudice to the Constitution establishing a different age for the latter in certain situations.

Article 60 provides that the law shall establish how persons deprived of their liberty may exercise their right to vote in an informed and voluntary manner.

Article 62 enshrines that when the people and the congress or president have a dissenting opinion, the decision of the people shall prevail and this decision shall be expressed through plebiscite. The parliamentarians and president are the representatives of the people and it is presumed that

that they carry the will of the electors, so it is rational and logical that the opinion of the people through a plebiscite is more important than that of their representatives.

Article 63 establishes the requirements to be President of the Republic. Among them, the differences with the current system are that the age is lowered to 30 years and that he or she must have higher education, either technical or university. In addition, the president may never be re-elected, whether for the next term or any future term, in order to avoid the accumulation of power in a single person and the capture of voters.

Article 64 stipulates that the president, parliamentarians and ministers may be constitutionally charged with the action of impeachment for having seriously violated the security of the State, the honour of the Nation in the eyes of international society or the people, and for having infringed or having caused the infringement of constitutional rights and guarantees. In this sense, this action may be brought not only when the subject has directly infringed constitutional rights, but also when, through him or her or through his or her orders or decisions, these have been violated. Furthermore, the person sanctioned by this action may not hold elected office for a period of 10 years, without prejudice to any other responsibilities for which he or she may be held accountable.

The quorum required to remove the president from office through constitutional impeachment is reduced, requiring an absolute majority of deputies and 4/7 of the senators in office. On the other hand, to remove a deputy or senator or a group of deputies or senators through constitutional impeachment, in addition to meeting the requirements, the votes of the absolute majority of deputies and senators in office and the favourable vote of the President of the Republic are required, but if the President does not approve, the action may be accepted if all the deputies in office insist with 4/7 of their votes.

It also provides for another way of carrying out such actions, which is in a trial before the Supreme Court, where due process, especially impartiality, will be guaranteed. The rationale behind this is that someone who is actually responsible should not be left unpunished, just because his or her political sector has a majority in congress and justice is enforced.

above all.

Article 65 modifies who is the Vice-President of the Republic, with ministers not being able to hold that position. The order is as follows: President of the Senate; President of the Chamber of Deputies; President of the Supreme Court; President of the Court of Appeals of Santiago.

Article 66 enshrines, among the functions of the president, that he may still make decrees with the force of law after delegation of the powers of Congress, as established by law.

Article 67 establishes that in order for the president to dissolve the Chamber of Deputies or the Senate, he must call a national plebiscite and be authorised to do so by the citizens, and that the vote will be mandatory for people between 18 and 60 years of age, without prejudice to those who have a serious health problem or other impediment established by law.

Article 68 states that the president may not receive or make donations without parliamentary authorisation.

In Article 69 of Chapter V a limitation is set for the election of ministers and that is that half of them must be elected from parliament under the justification that political powers should come as much as possible from the choice of the people.

Article 70 establishes new requirements to be a minister, such as being 25 years old, having higher technical or university studies and "that the degree obtained is in accordance with the subject matter of the minister's post, for example, that the minister covering education has studied basic pedagogy, kindergarten education or another career related to education; likewise, that the minister covering the area of health has studied medicine, nursing, nursing technician, obstetrics, among other careers related to the area of health, and in the same way with all ministerial posts".

Article 71 enshrines the power of the Chamber of Deputies to dismiss all Ministers of State with 4/7 of the votes. In addition, "the Chamber of Deputies may, with the vote of the absolute majority of its members in office, dismiss a particular Minister of State, when based on mismanagement of his or her portfolio or the causes named in Article 64 of the Constitution".

Chapter VI, Article 73 states that the number of deputies and senators shall be established by law.

Article 74 establishes that persons who have been convicted of corruption or other similar offences may not be deputies, senators, presidents, mayors or hold any other public office for at least 10 years, which may be extended by law. In addition, anyone convicted of such offences shall immediately leave office.

Article 76 establishes that senators will serve for only 4 years, down from the current 8-year term of office.

Article 77 provides that a member of parliament who is removed from office shall remain in office until the next member who replaces him or her is elected and that he or she shall remain in office until the time allotted to the member who was removed and shall not be eligible for re-election at the next election.

Article 79 states that no member of the armed forces or the police may be a member of parliament, nor may anyone who has ever been a member of parliament, but military service is not an impediment to being a member of parliament.

Article 84 states that a member of parliament may be expelled for disciplinary problems in relation to the rules they have. However, to remove a parliamentarian from office, a 2/3 vote of the chamber that is impeaching him or her is required, and that session is mandatory.

Article 86 establishes the possibility of a trial for the removal of a minister.

of the Supreme Court with 4/7 of the votes of both chambers and this trial will be regulated by law. The rationale for this is that the Supreme Court, although independent and autonomous, must have some kind of control and the motivation for the trial is not to remove judges for political reasons, but for particularly serious reasons such as, for example, prevarication.

Article 88 of Chapter VII stipulates that draft laws may be initiated in any of the chambers and by the President of the Republic, but only by the President of the Republic.

it will be up to parliament to vote on such bills due to the separation of state functions. In this sense, the manner of creation of the law is modified to one in which the legislative branch exercises the functions of a legislative branch and the executive branch does not interfere in its work, without prejudice to the exceptions that the Constitution itself enshrines. Without prejudice to this, the president may establish decrees with the force of law after the delegation of powers by Congress, as established by law. The popular initiative of law is also enshrined so that it is the citizens themselves who say what they want as a law, giving even more representativeness to our legal system, with those bills having to be voted on within 3 months of their presentation. Congress has the obligation to vote on these bills, not to approve them, but to discuss them.

Article 89 provides for the abolition of pardon as a real and effective demonstration of the separation of functions between the courts and the president.

Article 90 emphasises the fact that, with the mere approval of a bill by both chambers, it is ready to become law, without the need for a vote of the president.

Article 93 of Chapter VIII sets out with greater doctrinal clarity the definition of jurisdictional power and the powers possessed by the courts. It also establishes that there can be no courts outside the judiciary.

Article 96 establishes that the Supreme Court will be the body in charge of reviewing the constitutionality of any provision of the legal system, thus eliminating the constitutional court.

Article 97 establishes further requirements to become a lawyer, such as that the universities providing legal education must have high quality standards and that graduates must take an examination at the judicial academy before impartial doctors of law. The rationale for this is the need of society as a whole to have its interests and rights protected in the best possible way.

Chapter IV, Article 100 stipulates that local representatives shall remain at least 4 hours per day within the premises of their respective

institutions to be at the service of the community. The rationale for this is that there are many mayors or councillors who do not attend the respective municipality and when requested they are not available.

Article 102 enshrines the right of citizens in local communities to decide on their respective areas. In order for parliament to pass a law affecting a particular locality or public body, a plebiscite will need to be called to obtain the votes of those people granting approval.

Article 116 of Chapter XIV establishes the way to modify or change the Constitution for a new one. This will require the votes of 3/5 of the deputies and senators in office and then a plebiscite will be called for the citizens to decide whether they want a new Constitution or not, or whether they want to amend the Constitution or not. It also establishes the possibility that the text of the new Constitution, or the modification, will be established by the people through constituent assemblies, in accordance with the provisions of the law.

Article 120 stipulates that the Constitution shall be taught in secondary schools in the subject: "Civic Education" and that the minimum articles to be taught shall be fixed by law. However, Chapter I shall be compulsory, knowledge of fundamental rights and guarantees being an indispensable part of the training that any person should have in order to protect themselves and those around them.

Article 121 establishes that the institutions not expressly or tacitly repealed by a new Constitution shall be understood to remain in the legal system with merely legal status and that their subsequent amendment or repeal shall require a simple majority.

Political Constitution of the Republic of Chile

CHAPTER I. Fundamental rights and guarantees

The Chilean people recognises universal, inviolable, independent, indivisible and inalienable human rights as the foundation of every human community, of peace and justice in the world.

The following rights are therefore binding on the executive, legislative and jurisdictional functions, constituting a limitation on sovereignty.

All citizens shall be respected as individuals. Their right to life, liberty and the pursuit of happiness shall, so long as it does not interfere with the public welfare, be the supreme aim of legislation and other acts of government.

Everyone has the right to life and to life with dignity. The death penalty is prohibited.

Euthanasia and abortion may be established only by law, always taking into consideration human dignity.

Article 3. Everyone has the right to physical integrity. The application of any unlawful coercion or torture, as prescribed by the international treaties in force signed by Chile and by law, is prohibited.

Article 4. Everyone has the right to psychological integrity. The State shall endeavour to provide the means for the good mental health of its inhabitants.

The State recognises the right of everyone to the enjoyment of the highest attainable standard of mental health.

Article 5. Everyone has the right to be forgotten. Thus, everyone can demand de-indexing, i.e. the removal of his or her name and personal information from virtual search engines.

All individuals have the right to have their information removed from computer or virtual media and not to have it republished without their prior authorisation. Internet search engines must also remove links and information posted if they are offensive and image-related data, whether true or false.

Article 6. All persons are equal before the law.

Men and women are equal before the law. There are no privileged individuals or groups. The state shall promote the effective realisation of the equal rights of women and men and encourage the elimination of existing disadvantages.

Article 7. The law protects all persons equally in the exercise of their rights and the law protects all persons without discrimination. Any form of of arbitrary discrimination whether by any formal or informal authority and the law or by any other person.

No one shall be disadvantaged or favoured because of his or her sex, descent, race, colour, sexual orientation, language, nationality and origin, beliefs, property, religious or political opinions. No one shall be disadvantaged on account of any physical or mental handicap.

Persons belonging to ethnic, religious or linguistic minorities shall not be denied the right, in community with the other members of their group, to enjoy their own culture, to profess and practise their own religion and to use their own language.

Article 8. All forms of slavery are prohibited. Any slave who enters Chilean territory, whether by land, air, sea or diplomatic means, is immediately free and shall be protected by the State.

Everyone has the right to due process.

1. Everyone is entitled to a fair and prompt hearing within a reasonable time by a competent, independent and impartial tribunal, previously established by law, in the determination of any criminal charge against him or of his rights and obligations of a civil, labour, fiscal or any other nature.

2 Everyone charged with a criminal offence has the right to be presumed innocent until proved guilty according to law. During the proceedings, everyone is entitled, on an equal footing, to the following minimum guarantees:

a)   the right of the accused to be assisted free of charge by a translator or interpreter if he or she does not understand or speak the language of the court or tribunal;

b)   prior and detailed notice to the defendant of the accusation made;

c)   granting the defendant adequate time and facilities for the preparation of his defence;

d)   the right of the accused to be assisted by the defence counsel of his choice and to communicate freely and privately with his defence counsel;

e)   the unwaivable right to be assisted by a defence counsel provided by the State, if the accused does not defend himself or appoint a defence counsel within the time limit established by law, which shall be at no cost to the accused;

f)   the right of the defence to examine witnesses present in court and to obtain the attendance, as witnesses or experts, of other persons who may be able to shed light on the facts;

g)   the right not to be compelled to testify against oneself or to plead guilty;

h)   the right to appeal against the judgement before a higher judge or court. This right must be guaranteed not only in criminal proceedings, but also in any other proceedings; and

i)   right to be tried without undue delay.

3. The confession of the accused is only valid if it is made without coercion of any kind.

4. An accused person acquitted by a final judgment may not be retried on the same facts.

5. Criminal proceedings should be public, except to the extent necessary to preserve the interests of justice and the safety of the parties.

6. Criminal liability shall not be presumed by law.

7. No offence shall be punishable by any penalty other than that prescribed by a law published prior to its commission, unless a new law favours the offender.

8. No person shall be tried by special commissions but by a court established by law prior to the commission of the offence.

9. The State shall provide a lawyer free of charge to anyone who requires one, if he/she is not financially able to afford one himself/herself. This service provided will be oriented to any area of law such as civil, criminal, labour, administrative, constitutional or any other and will be directed both to legal representation in a trial and to provide advice.

10. The procedure applicable to minors for penal purposes shall take into account this circumstance and the importance of encouraging their social rehabilitation.

11. Where a final conviction has subsequently been reversed on the ground that a fact fully probative of a miscarriage of justice has occurred or has been discovered, or a person who has suffered punishment as a result of such a conviction is subsequently proved innocent, he shall be compensated according to law, unless it is proved that the failure to disclose the unknown fact in time is wholly or partly attributable to him.

Whenever someone is wrongfully convicted, the State must compensate the person concerned for any damage. Such compensation shall not only be due when the person concerned is wrongfully convicted.

The judgment was not only the result of malpractice, but also of any miscarriage of justice.

Any person may make a claim for reparations against the State or a public body, as provided by law, if he or she has suffered damages as a result of the unlawful acts of any public authority.

12. No one may be punished by a penalty that is not proportionate to the punishable conduct and the legal good affected.

Article 10. The State shall take the necessary measures to promote the social reintegration of convicted persons.

Article 11. Everyone has the right to freedom of movement. Any person may move from one place to another within the national territory, remain and reside therein, and enter and leave the same without any disturbance whatsoever on the part of the authority or private individuals, without prejudice to such limitations as may be established by law and without prejudice to third parties.

The right to liberty may only be deprived by law and only in cases where there are insufficient means of subsistence and, as a result, special burdens arise for the community, or when it is necessary to defend against a danger threatening the existence or the fundamental regime of freedom and democracy of the Nation, or to combat the danger of epidemics, natural catastrophes or particularly serious disasters, to protect young people from neglect or to prevent particularly serious criminal acts.

He may also be deprived of this right by arrest or detention ordered by the competent public official in accordance with the law. Any person caught in flagrante delicto may be arrested by any person for the purpose of bringing him before the competent authority so that, within 24 hours, he may be brought before the competent judge.

A person deprived of liberty may only be held in accordance with the law, in his or her home or in a public place designated for that purpose.

All persons deprived of their liberty have the right not to be held incommunicado. Any person may visit him or her, subject only to the limitations provided for by law.

The stripping of persons by the authority is prohibited in any detention and in any case while deprived of liberty.

The release of the accused shall always be granted, with the exception of the following cases, declared by the competent judge:

1) Their arrest or detention is necessary for the investigations;

2) Their arrest or detention is necessary for the safety of the victim; and

3) Detention or imprisonment is necessary for the security of society.

The confiscation of objects used for the commission of the offences may be ordered. The penalty of confiscation of property shall apply to unlawful associations.

The loss of pension rights may never be established as a penalty.

Article 12. The State guarantees the right to migrate.

Migrant workers and members of their families shall enjoy equality of treatment with nationals in relation to:

a) Access to educational institutions and services, subject to the admission requirements and other regulations of the institutions and services concerned;

b) Access to vocational guidance and placement services;

c) Access to vocational training and retraining services and institutions;

d) Access to housing, including social housing schemes, and protection against rent exploitation;

e) Access to health and social services, provided that the requirements for participation in the relevant schemes have been met;

f) Access to cooperatives and self-managed enterprises, without any change in their status as migrant workers and subject to the rules and regulations governing the bodies concerned; and

g) Access to and participation in cultural life.

Article 13. All persons have the right to assemble peacefully and without arms, without prior permission.

Meetings in places of public use such as squares, beaches, stadiums and streets may be restricted only by law. Such restrictions must be justified as necessary in a democratic society, in the interests of national security, public safety or public order, or to protect public health or morals or the rights and freedoms of others.

Article 14. All persons have the right to form and join associations.

Associations whose aims or activities are contrary to criminal law or which are directed against the constitutional order or against the idea of understanding between peoples are prohibited.

No one may be compelled to belong to an association.

In order to have legal personality, the association must be constituted in accordance with the law.

Article 15. Everyone has the right to health and medical care. Medical care in state or state-run medical establishments shall be free of charge.

Everyone shall have the right to choose the health care system of his or her choice, whether public or private.

The State recognises the right of everyone to the enjoyment of the highest attainable standard of physical health.

Concealing facts and circumstances that may create a danger to the life and health of the nation or a sector of the population entails the liability determined by law.

The State shall protect the healthy development of children.

The State shall provide for the prevention, treatment and control of epidemic, occupational and other diseases.

Everyone has the right to sport.
Everyone has **the** right to live in a pollution-free environment and the duty to preserve an adequate environment.

The State shall ensure the rational use of all natural resources in order to protect and improve the quality of life and to defend and restore the environment, relying on the indispensable collective solidarity. It is also the duty of the State to ensure that this right is not affected and to protect the preservation of nature.

For those who violate the provisions of the previous section, criminal or, as the case may be, administrative sanctions will be established in the terms established by law, as well as the obligation to repair the damage caused.

The law may establish specific restrictions on constitutional rights in order to protect the environment.

Everyone has the right to reliable information on the state of the environment and the right to compensation for damage to health or property caused by breaches of environmental protection law.

Everyone has the right to honour, to be honoured and to have his or her private life and that of those close to him or her, such as family and friends, protected.

Everyone has the right to his or her own image.

The law shall limit the use of information technology in order to guarantee the honour and personal and family privacy of citizens and the full exercise of their rights.

Everyone has the right to inviolability of his person, his home and all forms of private communication, and to personal and family secrecy. These rights may only be subject to exceptions, such as the search of property, the interception of communications or the opening of documents, in the cases and in the manner determined by this Constitution, the law and by judicial decision. Without prejudice to this, in cases of flagrante delicto, the home of the affected party may be entered in order to arrest the perpetrator, without the consent of the owner.

Everyone has the right to a decent and adequate habitat and housing of adequate size, hygiene and comfort, and which preserves personal privacy and family privacy.

Article 19. Everyone has the right to freedom of conscience, to manifest his or her beliefs and to worship freely, so long as these are not contrary to security, public order and do not disturb the rights of others.

Everyone is guaranteed the right not to profess any religion, to freely choose his or her beliefs, to hold and disseminate his or her religious and other convictions, and to act in conformity with them.

No religious organisation shall receive privileges from the State, nor shall it exercise political authority. No one shall be obliged to take part in religious acts, celebrations, rites or practices of any kind. The State and its agencies shall refrain from intervening in religious education and any other activity of this nature, being a secular State.

Article 20. Everyone shall have freedom of expression and therefore has the right to express their opinion by any means without prior censorship, without prejudice to the right to be held responsible for

offences committed in the exercise of this right. All censorship shall be prohibited, subject to the provisions of the following paragraph.

Propaganda or agitation inciting social, racial, national or conscientious hatred or hostility is not permitted. Propaganda for social, racial, national, religious or linguistic supremacy is prohibited.

No one may be compelled to express his or her opinions and convictions or to renounce them.

Everyone has the right to inform, subject to the limitations prescribed in the Constitution.

Article 21. The state guarantees the right to freedom of the press and freedom of information by radio, television and film, subject to the limitations prescribed in the previous article.

There shall be no state monopoly over the media.

Any person, natural or legal, offended or unjustly alluded to by any media has the right to have his or her statement, rectification or reply broadcast free of charge, under the same conditions in which the offensive or unjust message was broadcast, by the media in which the information was broadcast.

The State, universities and other persons or entities determined by law may establish, operate and maintain television stations. There shall be a National Television Council responsible for overseeing the proper functioning of this medium of communication, and a law with a qualified quorum shall determine the organisation and other functions and powers of the said Council.

Article 22. Everyone has the right to education.

The care and education of children is the right and duty of parents. Children shall enjoy the protection provided for in international agreements that safeguard their rights. Every child has the right, without discrimination on any ground such as race, colour, sex, language, religion, national or social origin, property or birth, sexual identity or orientation, to such measures of protection as are required by his or her status as a minor by the Convention on the Rights of the Child.

by his or her family, society and the State. Every child shall be registered immediately after birth and shall have a name. Children and adolescents shall be protected against economic and social exploitation. Their employment in work harmful to their morals and health, or in which their lives are endangered or their normal development is at risk, shall be punishable by law. The Constitution protects the rights of children and shall place special emphasis on their protection, welfare, happiness and self-fulfilment. Every child should learn the values of respect, helping the community and refraining from violence.

Education shall be directed to the full development of the human personality and the sense of its dignity, and shall strengthen the respect for human rights and fundamental freedoms. Education shall enable all persons to participate effectively in a free society, promote understanding, tolerance and friendship among all nations and among all racial, ethnic or religious groups.

Against the will of the persons authorised to bring them up, children may be separated from their families only by virtue of a law, when the persons authorised to bring them up fail in their duty or when, for other reasons, the children are in danger of being abandoned.

Kindergarten, basic and secondary education shall be compulsory and available to all free of charge in the institutions that the State must provide for all children and adolescents. In the case of secondary education, this shall be extended until the age of 21 in accordance with the law.

Secondary education in its different forms, including technical and vocational secondary education, shall be made generally available and accessible to all by all appropriate means.

Higher education shall be made equally accessible to all, on the basis of capacity, by whatever means are appropriate. Free higher education may be available.

The State shall encourage and intensify, as far as possible, fundamental education for those persons who have not received or completed a full course of basic education.

The State shall actively pursue the development of the school system at all levels of education, introduce an adequate scholarship system, and continuously improve the material conditions of the teaching staff.

The State respects the liberty of parents and, where applicable, legal guardians to choose for their children or wards schools other than those established by the State, provided that such schools meet such minimum educational standards as may be laid down or approved by the State, and to ensure that their children or wards receive such religious or moral education as may be in conformity with their own convictions.

Article 23. The State guarantees freedom of education.

Limitations to this right are public order, national security and respect for fundamental rights.

Education provided by public institutions shall be secular and officially recognised teaching shall not be directed towards the propagation of any partisan political tendency.

The State recognises the right of parents or legal guardians to teach their children or wards themselves, subject to such regulations as may be laid down by or under the law. Parents also have the right to choose their children's educational establishment.

Article 24. Everyone has the right to freedom of labour and its protection.

Everyone shall have the opportunity to earn a living by work freely chosen or accepted.

Everyone has the right to freely choose his or her profession and vocational training. The exercise of the profession may be regulated by law or by virtue of a law.

All persons have the right to remuneration for their work without discrimination of any kind and not less than that established by law, as well as the right to unemployment protection.

Wages, hours of work, rest and other conditions of work shall be determined by law. Children shall not be exploited.

Forced labour is permissible only in the case of judicially ordered deprivation of liberty.

No person shall suffer prejudice in his or her work or employment because of his or her origins, opinions or beliefs.

The right to strike shall be exercised within the framework of the laws that regulate it.

The State shall guarantee to all persons, especially children, mothers and older workers, protection for their health, material security, rest and leisure. All persons who, by reason of their age, physical or mental condition or economic situation, are unable to work, shall be entitled to receive from the State adequate means of subsistence.

The State shall establish a guaranteed minimum wage sufficient to meet the needs of the worker and his family.

Young people over the age of 18 who are not in education, who are fit for work, and who are in employment, are obliged to take care of their disabled parents. They may be exempted from this duty by a court decision, on grounds of justified.

The law shall guarantee the right to collective bargaining between workers' and employers' representatives and the binding force of agreements.

The State guarantees the right to strike. However, a strike may not be declared by those who, because of it, may seriously affect the security, health, economy of the country or the supply of the Nation.

Article 25. All workers have the right to form trade unions in the cases and forms established by law.

Everyone can defend their rights and interests through trade unions and can belong to the trade union of their choice.

Article 26. The State shall take special care to safeguard the economic and social rights of Chilean workers abroad and shall direct its policy towards their return.

Article 27. All employers have the right to free employment. This right may be limited by law so that, by a court decision, a person may be compelled to work when the worker has so agreed.

Article 28. Everyone has the right to food. The State shall take appropriate measures to ensure the realization of this right for those who do not have the means to secure it.

Article 29. Everyone has the right to water. The State shall ensure that there is a supply of safe drinking water available to all persons.

Drinking water supply companies may not interrupt or suspend the water service for non-payment in the event that the law provides that it is a remunerated service, without prejudice to the rights that they may assert in an executive or ordinary lawsuit, as established by law.

The rights of private individuals over waters, recognised or constituted in accordance with the law, shall confer on their holders the ownership thereof.

Article 30. The State guarantees the right to social security. The

State shall supervise this right.

Laws regulating this right shall have a qualified quorum. Compulsory contributions may be established by law.

The public authorities shall guarantee, by means of adequate and regularly updated pensions, the economic sufficiency of citizens in old age. Likewise, and independently of family obligations, they shall promote their welfare by means of a system of social services which shall attend to their specific problems of health, housing, culture and leisure.

In any case, the pensioner shall have the right of ownership of his contributions, which shall be regulated by law.

Older persons have the right to economic security and to housing and family and community living conditions that respect their personal autonomy and prevent and overcome their isolation or social marginalisation.

Article 31. All persons have the right to petition the authority, individually or collectively, on respectful and expedient terms.

Members of the Armed Forces or of the Corps subject to military discipline may exercise this right only on an individual basis and in accordance with the provisions of their specific legislation.

All persons have the right to peacefully petition for the redress of grievances, the removal of public authorities, the enactment, repeal or amendment of laws, ordinances or regulations, as well as for other matters, without this being a ground for discriminatory measures against the person making use of this right. This right shall be regulated by law.

Article 32. All persons have the right to admission to all public functions and jobs, with no other requirements than those imposed by the Constitution and the law.

Article 33. All persons have the right to equal distribution of taxes. This right shall be regulated by law.

All shall contribute to the support of public expenditure in accordance with their economic capacity by means of a fair tax system inspired by the principles of equality and progressiveness which, in no case, shall have a confiscatory scope. In no case shall the law establish unfair or disproportionate taxes that exceed fifty percent of people's income.

The taxes collected shall enter the patrimony of the Nation and may only be earmarked for a specific purpose when authorised by law to be used for national defence, and those taxes obtained through activities or goods of local significance may be applied by regional or communal authorities to finance development works, as established by law.

Article 34. All persons and the State have the right to free economic initiative, provided that such activity is not contrary to public order, national security, and the culture.

When the State carries out business activities, it shall not be governed by special rules, but shall be subject to the ordinary regulations for any company in the sector in which it is established. Exceptions to the regulation of certain state enterprises may be made by law, which must have a qualified quorum.

Article 35. The State guarantees the self-determination of peoples. The State shall protect the original peoples.

Article 36. The State guarantees the protection of culture and historical, archaeological and cultural heritage.

In the same way, the State protects the history and culture of existing and extinct native peoples of which there are still religious, architectural, cultural, archaeological or historical remains.

Article 37. All persons have the right to acquire ownership of all kinds of property, with the exception of national property for public use.

A law of qualified quorum may establish limitations or requirements for the acquisition of certain assets, based on the national interest.

Article 38. All persons have the right of ownership to use, enjoy and dispose of their tangible and intangible property both individually and jointly with other persons. The content of this right shall be determined by law.

All persons have the right of ownership over works of their intellectual and artistic creation for the time specified by law, which shall not be less than the lifetime of their creator.

Industrial property rights are also guaranteed for the period of time stipulated by law.

The right to inheritance is guaranteed.

No one may be deprived of their property and rights except for justified reasons of public utility or social interest, by means of the corresponding compensation and in accordance with the provisions of the law.

Expropriation is permitted only for reasons of the common good. It may be effected only by law or by virtue of a law establishing the manner and amount of compensation. Compensation shall be fixed with equitable consideration of the interests of the community and of those affected. In the event of a dispute over the amount of compensation, the ordinary courts shall have jurisdiction. In order to be able to take physical possession of the expropriated property, the compensation must first be paid in full.

Article 39. All politically persecuted persons have the right to asylum.

The competent authorities of the Republic shall always be empowered to grant asylum to any foreigner persecuted for his action in the cause of freedom or who requests the protection of the State for any other reason.

The rights enshrined in this Chapter may not be interpreted in such a way as to affect their essence or prevent their free exercise. In the same way, laws complementing or regulating constitutional guarantees or limits when authorised by constitutional mandate may not affect their essence or impose conditions, taxes or requirements which impede their free exercise.

Article 41. Action for protection. Anyone who, as a result of arbitrary or illegal acts or omissions, suffers deprivation, disturbance or threat to the legitimate exercise of the rights and guarantees enshrined in Articles 2; 3; 4, first paragraph; 5; 6; 7; 8; 9; 10; 12, paragraph second; 13; 14; 15; 16; 17; 17; 18; 19; 20; 21; 22; 22; 23; 24; 25; 26; 27; 28; 28; 29; 30; 31; 32; 33; 34;

35; 36; 37; 38; and 39, may appeal by himself or by anyone who wishes to defend the rights of the affected party, to the respective Court of Appeal, which shall immediately adopt the measures it deems necessary to re-establish the rule of law and ensure the due protection of the affected party, without prejudice to the other rights that he may assert before the corresponding authority or courts.

Article 42. Action for protection. Any individual who is arrested, detained or imprisoned in breach of the provisions of the Constitution or the laws may, either by himself or by anyone on his behalf, apply to the magistracy designated by law, in order that the latter may order the legal formalities to be observed and immediately adopt such measures as it deems necessary to re-establish the rule of law and ensure the due protection of the person concerned.

This magistracy may order the individual to be brought before it, and its decree shall be obeyed precisely by all those in charge of prisons or places of detention. On being informed of the facts, it shall order the immediate release of the individual, or shall have the legal defects remedied, or shall bring the individual before the competent judge, proceeding in all cases briefly and summarily, and either correcting the defects itself or informing the appropriate person so that they may be corrected.

The same remedy, and in the same manner, may be applied in favour of any person who unlawfully suffers any other deprivation, disturbance or threat to his right to personal liberty and individual security. In such cases, the respective magistrate shall order the measures indicated in the preceding paragraphs that he deems appropriate to re-establish the rule of law and ensure the due protection of the affected party.

CHAPTER II. Sovereignty

The Republic of Chile is a democratic, secular and social State governed by the rule of law, which upholds freedom, justice, equality and political pluralism as the highest values of its legal system.

Article 44. All State power emanates from the people. This power is exercised by the people through elections and voting and through special organs of the legislative, executive and judicial functions.

Article 45. The legislative and executive functions shall be subject to the constitutional order; the judicial function shall be subject to the law and the law.

Against anyone who attempts to eliminate this order, all Chileans have the right of resistance when no other recourse is possible.

The State shall protect life and animals through legislation and, in accordance with the law and the law, through the judiciary, taking into account its responsibility towards future generations, within the framework of the constitutional order.

Article 48. The exercise of sovereignty recognises as a limitation the respect for fundamental rights. It is the duty of the organs of the State to respect and promote such rights as are guaranteed by this Constitution, as well as by the international treaties signed by Chile and which are in force.

The fundamental rights set out in such international human rights treaties shall form an integral part of this Constitution.

The general rules of public international law are an integral part of domestic law. They take precedence over laws and directly create rights and obligations for the inhabitants of the national territory. Treaties concluded by Chile and established international law shall be faithfully observed and obeyed.

The Chilean State is unitary, decentralised and recognises the plurality of peoples within the Nation. It shall promote the local identification of each region and native people.

Article 50. All State organs and individuals shall respect and obey the Constitution. Any act that contravenes the Constitution is null and void and shall give rise to the responsibilities provided for by law.

Article 51. Political parties participate in the formation of the political will of the people, their foundation is free and their internal organisation must respond to democratic principles. Parties must publicly account for the origin and use of their resources, as well as their assets.

Parties which by their aims or by the behaviour of their members or adherents tend to distort or eliminate the fundamental regime of freedom and democracy, or to endanger the existence of the Republic of Chile, are unconstitutional. The Supreme Court shall decide on their constitutionality, without prejudice to the possibility of bringing the actions provided for in article 64. Those responsible shall be disqualified for life from being elected to popular office.

The national emblems are the national flag, the coat of arms of the Republic and the national anthem.

The mission of the Armed Forces, consisting of the Army, the Navy and the Air Force, is to guarantee the sovereignty and independence of Chile, to defend its territorial integrity, the borders of the Nation when required, and the constitutional order. The forces of law and order are the Carabineros and the Investigative Police.

Law enforcement officials shall be trained to a high standard, shall be fully acquainted with the fundamental rights of individuals and the legal regulations pertaining to their areas of competence, and shall undergo continuous education and training throughout the entire period of their duties, which shall be regulated by law or by virtue of a law.

When a natural disaster occurs or a particularly serious disaster occurs and in order to help, the President of the Republic may request the assistance of the Carabineros de Chile, the Investigative Police and institutions of other administrations, as well as the Armed Forces. On the fifth day after the deployment of the Armed Forces, the Parliament shall vote on whether to extend it for 5 more days and after that time the same procedure shall be followed. In the above-mentioned cases only the right contained in Article 13 may be restricted.

In the event of civil or internal war, the President of the Republic shall obtain authorisation from Parliament to deploy the armed forces for a period of 30 days, extendable for a further 15 days, and thereafter for a further 15 days. This authorisation may be revoked at any time by either parliament or the President of the Republic, and in any case shall be deemed to be revoked when the danger has ceased. In this state, the rights of freedom of movement, of assembly, of the inviolability of the home and of all forms of private communication and of property may be restricted or limited if requisitioning is strictly necessary, which shall be justly compensated thereafter.

In the event of external war or when national defence against enemy attack is imminent, the President of the Republic may decree the deployment of the Armed Forces with the approval of Parliament. When the situation irrecusably demands immediate action and there are insurmountable obstacles to a timely meeting of Parliament, or if deliberation is not possible for lack of a quorum, the President of the Republic may decree the deployment of the Armed Forces with the concurring votes of 2/3 of the Ministers of State. All matters relating to external war or national defence in the event of enemy attacks shall be regulated by law, which must be approved by a majority of 4/7 of both Houses.

A law of qualified quorum shall regulate the bases of military organisation and administration in accordance with the principles of this Constitution.

Article 54. It is incumbent upon the public authorities to promote the conditions for the real and effective freedom and equality of the individual and of the groups of which he or she forms part; to remove obstacles which prevent or hinder their full realisation and to facilitate the participation of all citizens in political, economic, cultural and social life.

The Constitution guarantees the principle of legality, the hierarchy of norms, the publicity of rules, the non-retroactivity of punitive provisions that are not favourable or that restrict individual rights, legal certainty, responsibility and the prohibition of arbitrariness of public authorities.

Article 55. The Chilean State shall aim to achieve peace and a development that allows a life of dignity for all people without distinction of any kind. Likewise, the State recognises that the rights to innovation and technological advances are indispensable for the progress of the Nation. The State must ensure a correct distribution of wealth with respect for human rights.

that the Constitution and the law provide for.

CHAPTER III. Nationality and political rights

Article 56. Persons born in Chilean national territory by land, air or sea or in Chilean diplomatic territory abroad are Chileans, as are the children, grandchildren and great-grandchildren of Chileans, foreigners who have obtained a letter of nationalisation in accordance with the law and stateless persons who enter Chilean territory, whose nationality must be applied for and shall be granted to them upon proof that they have no other nationality. All others are foreigners.

The concepts of Chilean and citizen are equivalent. There are no stateless persons in Chile.

A Chilean or citizen whose nationality has been denied may appeal to the Supreme Court within 60 days of the date on which his nationality was denied, so that the Court may hear the matter in plenary session and rule on the matter in accordance with the rules of sound judgment. It shall be understood that the affected party is Chilean until the matter is resolved.

Chileans shall have the right to vote once they have reached the age of 18. At the same age, the right to be elected in popular elections shall be acquired, except when the Constitution establishes a different age for a specific post. These rights shall be lost only when the individual has been convicted of the conduct established in the second paragraph of article 51, and the right to be elected in popular elections shall also be lost if the individual has been convicted of a crime punishable by affliction. **Article 60.** The law shall establish the manner in which persons deprived of their liberty shall will be able to exercise their right to vote and learn about the policy proposals of the various candidates in order to have an informed vote. Voting will also be voluntary for prisoners.

The State shall guarantee a public electoral system guarded by both the Armed Forces and the Carabineros de Chile in the manner established by the law regulating the electoral process, which shall have a qualified quorum.

When the decision of the people and that of the Legislative or Executive Function are in conflict, the will of the people shall prevail. The manifestation of this will shall be exercised by means of a plebiscite.

CHAPTER IV. President of the Republic

To be elected President of the Republic, a person must be a Chilean with the right to vote, not have been convicted of a crime punishable by imprisonment, be over thirty years of age and have completed higher technical and/or university studies in one of the institutions recognised by the State.

The President of the Republic shall be elected by universal, direct, free, free, voluntary, equal and secret suffrage.

The President of the Republic shall hold office for four years unless he is removed from office, in which case his successor shall succeed him for the unexpired term. In no case may the President of the Republic be re-elected, either for the following period or for any other period thereafter.

The Vice-President of the Republic shall exercise the functions of the dismissed President until the new President of the Republic is elected.

Article 64. The President, ministers, deputies and senators may be constitutionally impeached with the action of impeachment for having seriously violated the security of the State, the honour of the Nation before international society or the people, and for having infringed or having caused constitutional rights and guarantees to be infringed.

To bring an impeachment action, between 5 and 20 deputies or senators are required to submit the action in writing as required by law.

In either case, the Vice-President shall call for elections within 5 days of the dismissal, which shall be held within 60 days of the dismissal if that day is a Friday, and otherwise on the Friday immediately following the dismissal.

An impeachment action may be brought even 6 months after leaving office, but in such a case it will simply be called a constitutional impeachment.

The person sanctioned in accordance with these actions shall be barred from holding public office for a period of 10 years, without prejudice to any criminal, civil or other sanctions that may be brought against him or her. In the event of a new sanction by action of impeachment or constitutional accusation, he shall be sanctioned with disqualification from holding public office for life.

To remove the President of the Republic from office by means of an impeachment action or to sanction him by means of a constitutional impeachment, an absolute majority of the deputies in office and 4/7 of the senators in office is required.

In order to remove a deputy or senator or a group of deputies or senators from office by means of an impeachment action or to punish them by means of a constitutional impeachment, the number of signatures prescribed in the second paragraph of this Article is required to initiate the action,

and the votes of the absolute majority of deputies and senators in office and the vote of the President of the Republic. If the President votes against, it may be carried out if 4/7 of the deputies in office insist with the majority of their votes.

The impeachment action and the constitutional accusation may also be brought directly before the Supreme Court in a trial in which all guarantees of due process shall be respected. If brought in this way, the outcome shall be determined by the Court and not by the votes of the Deputies and Senators as provided for in the preceding paragraphs.

The Vice-President in the event of the removal of the President is the President of the Chamber of Senators. If he is absent, it is the President of the Chamber of Deputies. If the President of the Chamber of Deputies is absent, the President of the Supreme Court shall take the place of the President. In the absence of the latter, it is up to the president of the Court of Appeals of Santiago.

The President of the Republic, with the advice and approval of the Cabinet, shall perform the following acts of State for the benefit of the people:

1. Promulgation and enactment of amendments to the constitution, laws, decrees and treaties.

2. Convocation of either or both houses of parliament. Dissolution of the Chamber of Deputies.

3. Dissolution of the Senate.

4. Proclamation of general elections for members of parliament, in case of dissolution.

5. Confirmation of the appointment and removal of Ministers of State and other officials in accordance with the law.

6. To issue decrees with the force of law after delegation of the powers of Congress, as established by law.

7. Call for a plebiscite.

8. Issue regulations.

9. Concession of honours.

10. Reception of foreign ambassadors and ministers and appointment of ambassadors and diplomatic ministers.

Article 67. In order for the President of the Republic, with the advice and approval of the Cabinet, to be able to dissolve the Chamber of Deputies or the Senate, he must call a national plebiscite and the citizens must authorise him to carry out this act with the majority of their votes. The vote referred to in this Article shall be compulsory for persons entitled to vote between 18 and 60 years of age, except for those persons suffering from a serious health problem or some other impediment, which shall in any case be established by law.

No property may be donated to the President of the Republic, nor may he receive it or make donations, without the authorisation of Parliament.

On 1 June of each year, the President of the Republic shall give an account of the administrative and political state of the Nation to the Plenary Congress.

CHAPTER V. Ministers

Article 69. The Ministers of State, elected by the President of the Republic, shall be persons of his or her confidence whom he or she has appointed to hold such office. Within its guidelines, each minister directs the affairs of his or her own portfolio on his or her own responsibility.

The President will be held accountable for the actions of his hand-picked ministers.

The majority of its members must be elected from among the members of Parliament. The President of the Republic may dismiss Ministers of State at his own discretion.

Article 70. The requirements to be a minister are to be a Chilean national over 25 years of age, to have graduated from an institution of higher technical or university studies and that the degree obtained is in accordance with the subject covered by the post of minister, such as, for example, that the minister covering education has studied basic pedagogy, kindergarten education or another career related to education; Likewise, the minister covering the area of health should have studied medicine, nursing, nursing technician, obstetrics, among other health-related careers, and likewise for all ministerial positions.

The Chamber of Deputies may, by a vote of 4/7 of its members in office, dismiss all Ministers of State, and the President shall appoint others to replace them within 10 days.

The Chamber of Deputies may, with the vote of the absolute majority of its members in office, dismiss a particular Minister of State, when based on mismanagement of his or her portfolio or the causes named in Article 64 of the Constitution.

When a vacancy occurs in the office of President of the Republic, the Ministers of State shall immediately cease to hold office.

CHAPTER VI. Parliament

There shall be a Chamber of Deputies and a Chamber of Senators. Both Houses shall be composed of members elected to represent the people as a whole. The number of members of each House shall be fixed by law.

Deputies and Senators shall be elected by universal, direct, free, voluntary, equal and secret suffrage. They are the representatives of the people as a whole, not bound by mandates or instructions, and subject only to their conscience.

The regulation of their elections shall be established by law, which, in any case, must have a qualified quorum.

Persons who have been convicted of corruption or other offences of a similar nature shall not be eligible to run for public office for a period of time established by law, which may not be less than 10 years. A public official convicted of such offences shall immediately cease to hold office.

The term of office of members of the Chamber of Deputies shall be four years. However, the term shall be terminated before its normal period when it is declared dissolved.

The term of office of members of the Chamber of Senators shall be four years and they shall be elected in the same elections as Deputies and the President of the Republic. However, the term shall be terminated before the end of their normal term when the Chamber of Senators is declared dissolved.

When a Member of Parliament is removed from office, he or she shall remain in office until a new Member of Parliament is elected. The Member elected in his place shall remain in office until the end of the term of office of the first Member of Parliament and shall not be eligible for election at the next succeeding election.

No person may be a member of both Houses at the same time or hold any other popularly elected office. An elected Member of Parliament or Senator shall cease to hold his or her former office incompatible with full office from the time of his or her election.

Deputies or senators may not represent anyone as a lawyer in any lawsuit, and those who do so shall cease to hold office. However, they may give classes on matters related to their technical or university profession in secondary schools and universities, respecting the requirements established by law for such work.

No individual belonging to the armed forces, the military or the police may hold any office in parliament.

No person shall be eligible to hold any office in parliament who has ever been a member of the institutions mentioned in the preceding paragraph. Military service does not render a person ineligible to hold any office in parliament.

Article 80. Deputies and Senators shall enjoy inviolability for opinions expressed in the exercise of their functions during speeches, debates or votes cast within the sessions of Parliament or its committees. This shall not apply to slanderous offences.

Article 81. When the Chamber of Deputies or Senators is dissolved, there shall be an general election of the members thereof within 40 days of the date of dissolution if that day is a Friday and if not on the Friday immediately following, and the full Parliament shall be convened within 30 days after the date of the election.

While the Chamber of Deputies is dissolved, the Chamber of Senators shall not sit. However, the Executive may, in the event of a national emergency, summon the dissolved Chamber of Deputies to an emergency session.

The measures adopted at the session referred to in the preceding paragraph shall be provisional, and shall be considered null and void, unless the new members of the Chamber of Deputies approve them within 10 days of the beginning of the next session.

No House may deliberate or resolve any matter without the presence of at least one-third of the totality of its members. All matters shall be decided in each House by a majority of the members present, with the exceptions provided for in the Constitution, and in the event of a tie, the Speaker of the respective House shall decide by his vote.

Article 83. The deliberations of both chambers shall be public. However, secret sittings may be held if at least two-thirds of the members present so decide. Each House shall keep a record of sittings. This register shall be published and distributed without transcription of those parts of secret sittings which so require. In the minutes of business transacted, the votes of Members shall be recorded if one-fifth or more of the Members present so request.

Each Chamber shall elect its own President and other authorities. It shall also establish its own rules of procedure with regard to meetings, procedures and internal discipline, and may sanction its members for disorderly conduct. However, in order to

The expulsion of a member on disciplinary grounds shall require a resolution to that effect passed by a two-thirds majority of the members of the House as a whole. Such a meeting shall be mandatory for the House.

Article 85. Ministers may, at any time, attend the sessions of both Houses, whether or not they are members thereof, for the purpose of dealing with the bills under discussion. They shall also attend when their presence is required for the purpose of giving reports or explanations.

Article 86. The Congress shall organise a procedural court consisting of members of both Houses to try the judicial magistrates of the Supreme Court against whom removal proceedings have been instituted on particularly serious grounds. The removal of a Supreme Court judge requires a 4/7 vote of the total number of members of each House. Other matters relating to impeachment shall be established by law.

Article 87. The Chambers may receive individual and collective petitions, always in writing, and direct submission by citizens' demonstrations is prohibited.

The Houses may refer to the Government the petitions they receive. The Government is obliged to explain its contents whenever the Houses so request.

CHAPTER VII. Creation of the law

Bills may be initiated in the Chamber of Deputies, the Chamber of Senators and by the President of the Republic.

The President of the Republic may only initiate bills; he may not vote on them, and this task corresponds to the Congress in its capacity as the Legislative Power, with only the exceptions stipulated in the Constitution.

The President of the Republic may only issue decrees with the force of law after having delegated the powers of Congress, as established by law.

Citizens will also have a popular initiative, being able to present legal initiatives through a lawyer, subscribed by at least 1,000 citizens.

Legal initiatives or bills submitted by the people may not be shelved and shall be voted on within three months of their submission to the Chamber of Deputies.

Laws with a qualified quorum and those interpreting the Constitution shall require, for their approval, modification or repeal, an absolute majority of Deputies and Senators in office. Other laws shall require a simple majority of the Deputies and Senators present, without prejudice to the exceptions and other requirements established by this Constitution.

Article 89. In the Republic of Chile there is no pardon, in accordance with the principle of independence and autonomy of the functions of the State.

Article 90. A bill, when passed by both Houses, is ready to become a law after having been sanctioned, promulgated and published, except in the cases of exception provided for in the Constitution. The bill, when initiated by Congress, is called a motion.

When a bill passed by the Chamber of Deputies is rejected by the Senate, it shall become law if the Chamber of Deputies insists with a majority of at least two-thirds of the members present.

The provisions of the preceding paragraph do not prevent the Chamber of Deputies from convening a joint committee of both Houses, in the manner provided for by law.

If the Senate does not take a final decision within 60 days after receiving a bill passed by the Chamber of Deputies, except during the recess period, the Chamber of Deputies may consider the bill as passed by the Senate.

The President of the Republic may initiate a bill by means of a message, which shall be voted on, firstly by the Chamber of Deputies, then by the Chamber of Senators, and finally, if it has been approved by both or as stipulated in the preceding Article, it shall return to the President of the Republic for his sanction and promulgation.

When a bill passed by the Chamber of Senators is rejected by the Chamber of Deputies, it shall become law if the Chamber of Deputies insists with a majority of at least two-thirds of the members present.

If a bill passed by the Chamber of Senators is rejected by at least two-thirds of the Chamber of Deputies, it shall be deemed to have been totally rejected, with no possibility of being passed at a later date.

CHAPTER VIII. Jurisdictional Function

Article 93. Jurisdictional power is a derivation of State sovereignty that places the subject agent in a position of superiority in relation to the subjects of law that relate to it, which is satisfied by applying objective law to the specific case to be dealt with.

request of a party, with objective disinterestedness and irrevocable action in law.

The power to hear civil and criminal cases, to judge them and to enforce judgments belongs exclusively to the courts established by law. When they have been called upon to act in a lawful manner and in matters within their jurisdiction, they may not be excused from exercising their authority even in the absence of a law settling the dispute submitted to their decision.

The judicial function shall be exercised exclusively by the Supreme Court, the Courts of Appeal and the lower courts, as established by law.

There shall be no extraordinary courts outside the Judiciary, and no organ of the Executive shall have final judicial powers.

Judges shall be limited only by this Constitution, the law and the orders issued by the Supreme Court.

Article 94. Judges shall be irremovable, except by public trial, unless they are judicially declared mentally or physically incapacitated for the performance of their duties. The law shall determine the age limit beyond which judges shall retire. No body of the Executive or the Legislature shall take disciplinary action against judges, without prejudice to the provisions of Article 86 of this Constitution.

Article 95. The law shall regulate the appointment of judges, which shall be by qualified quorum.

All judges shall receive adequate compensation from time to time, which shall not be diminished during their tenure of office.

To be a judge of the Supreme Court, you must be a lawyer with more than fifteen years of effective work experience in any area of law, have a good conduct, and have a good knowledge of the law.

irreproachable, not being affiliated to any political party and having stood out in the professional, university or research area.

The Supreme Court is the final court to determine the constitutionality of any law, ordinance, regulation or provision.

Article 97. To become a Lawyer of the Republic it is required to have studied a Bachelor's Degree in Legal and Social Sciences, or whatever name is given to it by the respective institution, in one of the Universities recognised by the State, those graduates must pass a degree examination at the Judicial Academy before Doctors of Law who must be impartial and those universities must possess an optimum quality index.

This provision shall be non-retroactive.

Article 98. Proceedings shall be public, as shall judgments. When a court unanimously decides that publicity may be dangerous to public order or morals, the proceedings may be conducted secretly, but trials for political offences, press offences or those in which the rights of the people guaranteed in Chapter I of this Constitution are in question shall always be conducted publicly. Likewise, trials in family matters may be conducted secretly.

CHAPTER IX. Local self-government

Article 99. Matters concerning the organisation and functioning of local public bodies shall be established by law, based on the principle of local self-government.

Article 100. Local public bodies shall establish assemblies as their deliberative bodies, as determined by law.

The executive officers of local public bodies, the members of their assemblies and other local authorities determined by law shall be elected by direct popular vote within their own communities.

Local public bodies must always be at the disposal of their community and shall have at least four hours a day within their respective institutions in order to receive people who wish to communicate messages to them, without prejudice to the rest days and training that representatives may have. To this end, the times and means by which citizens may communicate with them shall be established by law.

Article 101. Local public bodies shall have the right to manage their property, affairs and administration and to issue their own regulations within the limits of the law.

Parliament may not make laws applicable only to a public body without the consent of the majority of the voters of the public body concerned, obtained in accordance with the requirements of the law.

Laws cannot be made applicable only to a specific region, commune or sector without the consent of the majority of voters in that area.

CHAPTER X. Central Bank

Article 103. There shall be the institution of the Central Bank of Chile, the purpose of which shall be to promote the orderly and progressive development of the national economy and of credit which, while avoiding inflationary or depressive tendencies, shall permit the greatest possible use of the productive resources of the country. This institution shall be regulated by a law with a qualified quorum.

CHAPTER XI. Public Prosecutor's Office

Article 104. An autonomous, hierarchical body, known as the Public Prosecutor's Office, shall exclusively direct the investigation of the facts constituting an offence, those that determine punishable participation and those that prove the innocence of the accused and, where appropriate, shall exercise public criminal prosecution in the manner provided for by law. It shall also be responsible for taking measures to protect victims and witnesses. In no case may it exercise jurisdictional functions.

The offended party and other persons determined by law may also bring criminal proceedings.

The Public Prosecutor's Office may issue direct orders to the Law Enforcement and Security Forces during the investigation. However, actions that deprive the accused or third parties of the exercise of the rights guaranteed by this Constitution, or restrict or disturb them, shall require prior judicial approval. The requested authority shall comply with such orders without further formality and may not qualify their basis, timeliness, justice or legality, except by requiring the production of prior judicial authorisation, as the case may be.

Article 105. The law shall determine the organisation and powers of the Public Prosecutor's Office,

The Constitution shall establish the qualifications and requirements that prosecutors must have and fulfil in order to be appointed and the grounds for removal of deputy prosecutors, where not provided for in the Constitution. Persons appointed as prosecutors may not have any impediment that would disqualify them from holding the office of judge. Regional and deputy prosecutors shall cease to hold office when they reach 75 years of age.

The law shall establish the degree of independence and autonomy and the responsibility that prosecutors shall have in the direction of the investigation and in the exercise of public criminal action, in the cases they are in charge of.

The National Public Prosecutor shall be appointed by the President of the Republic, at the proposal of the Supreme Court and with the agreement of the Senate adopted by two thirds of its members in office, in a session specially convened for this purpose. If the Senate does not approve the proposal of the President of the Republic, the Supreme Court shall complete the quine by proposing a new name to replace the rejected one, repeating the procedure until an appointment is approved.

The National Public Prosecutor must have at least ten years of law degree, be at least forty years of age and possess the other qualifications required to be a citizen with the right to vote; he shall serve for a term of eight years and may not be appointed for the following term.

The age limit for judges shall apply to the National Public Prosecutor.

Article 107. There shall be a Regional Public Prosecutor in each of the regions into which the country is administratively divided, unless the population or geographical extension of the region makes it necessary to appoint more than one.

The regional prosecutors shall be appointed by the National Prosecutor, on the proposal of the Court of Appeal of the respective region. In the event that there is more than one Court of Appeal in the region, the shortlist shall be formed by a joint plenary meeting of all of them, specially convened for this purpose by the President of the Court of the oldest Court of Appeal.

Regional prosecutors must have at least five years of law degree, have

They shall serve for eight years and may not be appointed as regional prosecutors for the following period, which does not prevent them from being appointed to another position in the Public Prosecutor's Office.

Article 108. The Supreme Court and the Courts of Appeal, as the case may be, shall call for a public competition of antecedents for the composition of the lists and shortlists, which shall be decided by the absolute majority of their members in office, in a plenary session specially convened for this purpose. Active or retired members of the Judiciary shall not be eligible to sit on the lists and shortlists.

The lists and shortlists shall be drawn up in a single ballot in which each member of the plenary shall be entitled to vote for three or two persons respectively. Those obtaining the first five or the first three majorities, as appropriate, shall be elected. In the event of a tied vote, the tie shall be broken by the drawing of lots.

Article 109. There shall be deputy prosecutors who shall be appointed by the National Public Prosecutor, on the proposal of the respective regional prosecutor on a shortlist of three candidates, which shall be drawn up after a public competition, in accordance with the constitutional organic law. They shall be qualified as lawyers and possess the other qualifications required to be citizens with the right to vote.

The National Public Prosecutor and the regional public prosecutors may only be removed by the Supreme Court for incapacity, misconduct or manifest negligence in the exercise of their functions. The Court shall hear the matter in a plenary session specially convened for this purpose and, in order to agree on the removal, it shall require the affirmative vote of the majority of its members in office.

The removal of regional prosecutors may also be requested by the National Prosecutor.

The National Public Prosecutor shall have the directive, correctional and economic superintendence of the Public Prosecutor's Office, in accordance with the respective law.

CHAPTER XII. Electoral Service

Article 112. An autonomous body, with its own legal personality and assets, called the Electoral Service, shall be responsible for the administration, oversight and supervision of the electoral and plebiscite processes; compliance with the rules on transparency, limits and control of electoral expenditure; the rules on political parties, and other functions established by a constitutional organic law.

The top management of the Electoral Service shall be vested in a Board of Directors, which shall exercise exclusively the powers entrusted to it by the Constitution and the law. This Council shall be made up of five councillors appointed by the President of the Republic, subject to the agreement of the Senate, adopted by two thirds of its members in office. The term of office of the Councillors shall be ten years, they may not be appointed for a further term and they shall be renewed every two years.

Councillors may only be removed by the Supreme Court for serious infringement of the Constitution or the laws, incapacity, misbehaviour or manifest negligence in the exercise of their functions. The Court shall hear the matter in plenary session, specially convened for this purpose, and in order to agree on the removal, it must obtain the affirmative vote of the majority of its members in office.

The organisation and powers of the Electoral Service shall be established by law. Its form of deconcentration, staffing levels, remuneration and staff regulations shall be established by law.

CHAPTER XIII. Office of the Comptroller General of the Republic

Article 113. An autonomous body to be known as the Office of the Comptroller General of the Republic shall exercise control over the legality of acts of government and administration, oversee the income and investment of the funds of the Treasury, of local public bodies or municipalities, assemblies, Deputies and Senators and of the other bodies and services determined by law; it shall examine and judge the accounts of persons in charge of the assets of these bodies; it shall keep the general accounts of the Nation, and shall perform such other functions as may be entrusted to it by the respective constitutional organic law.

The Comptroller General of the Republic shall have at least ten years of law, shall be at least forty years of age and shall possess the other qualifications required to be a citizen with the right to vote. He shall be appointed by the Supreme Court for a period of eight years and may not be appointed for the following period. However, on reaching the age of 75 years, he shall cease to hold office. The Court shall hear the matter in a plenary session, specially convened for this purpose, and in order to agree on the removal, it must obtain the assent of the majority of its members in office.

In the exercise of the function of control of legality, the Comptroller General shall take note of the decrees and resolutions which, in accordance with the law, must be processed by the Office of the Comptroller General or shall represent that they may be illegal; but he shall act on them when, in spite of his representation, the President of the Republic insists on the signature of all his Ministers, in which case he shall send a copy of the respective decrees to the Chamber of Deputies. In no case shall he give effect to decrees

of expenditure in excess of the limit laid down in the Constitution and shall forward a full copy of the record to the same House.

The Comptroller General of the Republic shall also be responsible for reviewing decrees having the force of law, and shall represent them when they exceed or contravene the law.

delegatory or contrary to the Constitution.

If the representation takes place with respect to a decree with force of law, a decree promulgating a law or a constitutional reform for departing from the approved text, or a decree or resolution for being contrary to the Constitution, the President of the Republic shall not have the power to insist, and if he is not satisfied with the representation of the Comptroller's Office, he shall refer the background to the Supreme Court within ten days, in order for it to resolve the controversy.

Otherwise, the organisation, functioning and powers of the Office of the Comptroller General of the Republic shall be the subject of a law, which shall require a majority of 4/7 of the Deputies and Senators in office.

The Office of the Comptroller General of the Republic shall also oversee the legality of the acts of the members of the Chamber of Deputies and the Chamber of Senators. In addition, the Comptroller General may impose fines and shall only reduce the salaries of such members when they have been absent from sessions without real medical justification or when they are not actually performing their parliamentary duties outside Parliament, and such reduction in their salaries shall be in proportion to the days not worked.

CHAPTER XIV. Amendments

Amendments or modifications to this Constitution must be approved in Parliament by the concurring vote of at least three fifths of the total membership of each House and then submitted for ratification by the people, who must approve them by a majority of the votes cast in a special plebiscite or in an electoral act to be determined by Parliament. The text of the amendment or change of the Constitution may be established through constituent assemblies, as established by law. From part of the Constitution may be amended or replaced by a new Constitution.

Amendments or modifications so ratified shall be promulgated forthwith by the President of the Republic in the name of the people as an integral part of this Constitution. Likewise, the change of the Constitution so ratified shall be promulgated forthwith by the President of the Republic on behalf of the people.

CHAPTER XV. Supreme Law

The fundamental human rights guaranteed by this Constitution to the people of Chile are the fruit of the ancient human struggle for freedom, have survived numerous severe trials over time, and are entrusted to these and future generations to guard them permanently and inviolably.

Article 118. This Constitution shall be the supreme law of the Nation and no law, ordinance, decree having the force of law or other act of government or any other act of government, in whole or in part, contrary to the provisions of this Constitution, shall have any legal force or validity.

The President of the Republic, as well as Ministers of State, members of Parliament, judges and all other public authorities, have the obligation to respect and defend this Constitution. Failure to comply with this provision shall lead to removal from office and the other sanctions or penalties established by the Constitution and the law.

This Constitution of the Republic shall be taught in public and public schools during secondary education through the subject: "Civic Education", and the minimum articles to be taught shall be established by law, among which must be found the

Chapter I in its entirety.

Article 121. The chapters in which institutions are regulated by the Constitution, which are not expressly or tacitly repealed by the new Constitution, shall be understood to remain in the legal system with their respective regulation as if they were a law, and their amendment or repeal shall require a simple majority of the votes of Deputies and Senators.

CHAPTER XVI. Supplementary provisions

This Constitution shall enter into force on the first day after the expiry of six months from the date of its promulgation.

The enactment of the laws necessary for the entry into force of this Constitution, the election of the members of the Houses, the procedure for the convocation of Parliament and the other preparatory procedures necessary for the entry into force of this Constitution may be carried out before the day specified in the preceding paragraph.

If the Chamber of Senators has not been constituted before the entry into force of this Constitution, the Chamber of Deputies shall function as a full parliament until the Chamber of Senators is constituted.

Ministers of State, members of the Chamber of Deputies and judges in office at the time this Constitution enters into force, as well as other public authorities holding offices recognised by this Constitution, shall not cease to hold office on account of the entry into force of this Constitution, unless so specified by law. Where, however, successors are appointed or elected in accordance with the provisions of the Constitution, they shall not cease to hold office on account of the entry into force of this Constitution, unless so specified by law.

shall be automatically removed from office.

Table of Contents

Printed by Books on Demand GmbH, Norderstedt / Germany